CW01302411

© 2022 Tony Raphaël

Tony Raphaël

The Essentials of Speed Reading :
Proven techniques
to read faster and understand better

Independently published

ISBN: 9798376654293

The Code of the intellectual property authorizing, under the terms of the paragraphs 2 and 3 of the article L.122-5, on the one hand, only the "copies or reproductions strictly reserved for the private use of the copyist and not intended for a collective use" and, on the other hand, that the analyses and the short quotations with an aim of example or illustration, "any representation or reproduction in whole or in part made without the assent of the author or his successors in title or assigns is illicit" (article L.122-4). This representation or reproduction, by any means whatsoever, would constitute an infringement punishable by articles L.335-2 and following of the Code of intellectual property.

Tony Raphaël

The Essentials of Speed Reading :
Proven techniques to read faster and understand better

Independently published

The Essentials of Speed Reading :
Proven techniques to read faster and understand better
TONY RAPHAËL

Table of content

Chapter 1 : Prerequisite   9

I. Why a book on speed reading?   9

II. Speed reading: what it is and how it can help you 15

III. Qualities required to master speed reading   21

IV. Prerequisites to improve your understanding   25

V. Eye functioning in reading   35

Chapter 2 : Basics   39

VI. Speed reading: 10 basics point   39

VII. Working on your technique   69

Chapter 3 : Next level   87

VIII. Optimize your reading speed   87

IX. Speed Reading and Decision Making   91

What is next?   *101*

CHAPTER 1 : PREREQUISITE

I. Why a book on speed reading?

Are you ready to revolutionize your approach to reading and optimize your performance? This book provides the essentials to master speed reading, achieve your reading goals, and, most importantly, understand the critical points while staying motivated. Before we dive into this exciting topic, let me share my journey with you.

I have always had a hard time enjoying reading. This was a source of difficulty for me during my studies, as I needed help learning and revising my courses properly. However, I needed to succeed in my studies, so I tried to read as quickly as possible to assimilate the knowledge I was missing. Unfortunately, my efforts were in vain, and I could not understand what I was reading.

When I was trying to review philosophy classes, I couldn't follow the authors' complex reasoning and retain the information. Similarly, when I had to read a novel in French, I found it boring and couldn't get into the story.

After many months of research, I finally understood my problem: I could not understand the texts I was reading, and my reading speed was below average. That's when I discovered the speed-reading technique. I learned that I could not only understand better but also faster. So I spent my time learning how to read correctly and how the eyes work, and eventually, I finished third in my class.

Today, my goal is to share my experience through a book. I hope interested people can discover speed reading techniques from the beginning of their studies, so they don't have to waste months looking for them like I did. This will save them time and make them more successful in their studies.

For example, thanks to speed reading, I could read philosophy books in half of the time and understand them better. Similarly, I could read French novels with more pleasure and retain the story's details better. I am confident that these techniques will benefit everyone, and I hope my book can help many students improve their reading and comprehension of texts. It saves time and helps them improve their studies while enjoying reading more.

Since I discovered the speed-reading technique and put the tips I learned into practice, I noticed that many people around me also had difficulties with reading. So, I decided to share my information with them and was delighted to find it beneficial.

I met a co-worker who needed help reading and understanding instructions for a project. I advised him to practice the speed-reading techniques I had learned, and after a few weeks of practice, he told me that it made a huge difference for him. He could read and understand instructions much faster, which helped him be more organized and get the job done.

I also met a friend who was preparing for an exam and needed help reading and retaining information. I advised her to practice speed reading techniques, and she told me it was beneficial. She could read and understand the texts she had to learn much faster and passed her exam with flying colors.

These examples show the importance of learning and discovering techniques to understand information better. Speed reading is a handy technique that can help people improve their learning and success, regardless of their area of interest or goal. That is why it can benefit everyone, and I hope my book can help many students and professionals improve their reading and comprehension of texts. I want my book to be a source of motivation for anyone who wants to enhance their learning and success, and reading can be a valuable tool in achieving this goal.

This book is intended to teach you to speed reading techniques and tips for improving your comprehension and recall of texts. However, it is essential to note that speed reading is a technique that requires practice and training to be implemented effectively. So, just as a book on swimming alone is not enough to know how to swim, the same is true for this book and speed reading. To improve your reading and comprehension, practicing the tips and techniques in this book with the key concepts in mind is essential.

It's important to realize that you will need more than just reading books about speed reading to improve. The real key to success in our industry is persistent, committed practice. You must take the time to read this book more than once, not just once. By doing so, you can be sure that you fully comprehend the strategies and advice provided and that you can use them to your advantage every day.

Regarding speed reading, the adage "practice makes perfect" couldn't be more applicable. You must actively put the techniques into practice whenever you have the chance rather than just reading about them. Take advantage of every chance to practice your newfound abilities, whether reading a chapter in a book, an article in the newspaper, or even a quick email. The more you use the tactics, the more at ease and natural they'll feel, resulting in genuine advancement and improvement.

The secret to accomplishing your speed reading objectives is consistency. Do your best to incorporate the tactics into your regular activities and keep going immediately if you notice any changes. Even though the differences might not be apparent immediately, they eventually become clear. You'll read more quickly and be able to read and understand materials more quickly and effectively.

Do not be afraid to keep trying and keep practicing. Remember that perseverance pays off, and the outcomes will be more than worthwhile. Consistent practice can help you achieve your goals, whether to read more books, read at work more quickly, or simply to wow your loved ones with your improved reading abilities. Make the commitment, put in the position, and you'll soon see the value of your persistence!

CHAPTER 1 : PREREQUISITE

II. Speed reading: what it is and how it can help you

Have you ever thought about how much time you spend reading every day? Reading emails, online articles, books, and reports for work may take up much time, and before you realize it, your entire day has passed. But consider what you could do with all that time if you invested it wisely. Imagine being able to read more quickly, effectively, and comprehensively. It could have a significant effect on both your personal and professional life.

It is obvious what advantages quick reading has. You can increase your knowledge and maintain awareness of a wide range of topics by reading more quickly and through more material in less time. This can be especially helpful in a professional setting where you must read and comprehend reports and paperwork swiftly. Gaining efficiency and productivity through fast reading will put you ahead of the competition.

Consider all the novels you've longed to read but have never found the time. Think about how many more you could read if you could read them more quickly and with better comprehension. Reading should be a tool for learning and development rather than idle time. You can turn every minute you spend reading into a worthwhile investment in yourself if you learn the skill of fast reading.

Refrain from allowing time to stand in the way of your achievement and development. It's up to you to make the most of every minute since they all count. You can save time, increase your knowledge, and create new opportunities for growth and development through speed reading. So don't wait; get started immediately on your path to a faster, more compelling reading.

Fortunately, there is a reading technique that allows you to do just that: speed reading. Speed reading will enable you to read faster while maintaining a good understanding of what you're reading. This means you can read more in less time while understanding what you're reading better. It's a valuable skill that can help you succeed in all aspects of your life, whether it's work, school, or personal life.

Speed reading is a technique that allows you to read faster while maintaining a good understanding of what you are reading. This means you can read more in less time while understanding what you are reading better. This technique is handy and can help you save time, understand the texts you read better, and remember them more easily.

Imagine how much time you could save each day if you read faster. You could read in-depth articles in less time, understand your boss's emails better, and even finish your vacation books more quickly. And that's not all! Speed reading also helps you better understand the text you read, which means you'll be able to retain the information better and use it more effectively. Thanks to the speed-reading technique, you'll even be able to remember it more easily.

The origins of speed reading go back many centuries. As early as antiquity, Greek philosophers such as Plato and Aristotle developed speed reading techniques to understand better and retain their peers' writings. Since then, the speed-reading technique has been perfected over the centuries.

During the eighteenth century, many thinkers and educators began to focus on speed reading and to study its effects on learning and comprehension. One of the first to truly popularize the speed-reading technique was the French writer and philosopher Voltaire, who used speed reading to quickly read and comprehend large amounts of text.

In the 20th century, speed reading became increasingly popular thanks to educators such as Evelyn Wood and Tony Buzan. Wood developed a speed-reading method based on eye movement and keyword recognition. At the same time, Buzan popularized speed reading by using memorization and visualization techniques to help people read faster and better understand what they read.

Speed reading is a technique that has been developed and perfected over the centuries, but it has become prevalent in recent years. But why? What has led to this increased popularity of speed reading in recent years?

There are several reasons why speed reading has become so popular in recent years. First, we live in a world where information is everywhere. We are constantly bombarded with emails, articles, notifications, and messages. To keep up, we need ways to read faster and better understand what we are reading. Speed reading allows us to do just that.

In addition, speed reading has become popular in recent years because it can be used in many different contexts. Whether you are a student, a professional, or just someone who likes to read, speed reading can help you achieve your goals faster and more efficiently. It can help you learn more quickly, understand what you read, and remember it more easily.

Finally, speed reading has become popular in recent years thanks to the many tools and resources available for those who want to learn this skill. Whether you prefer books, videos, or online courses, there are plenty of ways to learn speed reading and become a pro.

But how does speed reading work? And how can you use it to improve your daily life? This book will explore the basics of speed reading and show how this technique can help you achieve your goals. We'll look at how to use speed reading to learn faster, solve problems more effectively, and make better decisions more quickly.

Speed reading is a valuable skill that can help you succeed in all aspects of your life. So, ready to discover the secrets of speed reading and become a reading pro? Let's get started!

CHAPTER 1 : PREREQUISITE

III. What are the qualities required to master speed reading?

Mastering speed reading requires specific qualities and skills that can be developed and improved over time. Here are some of the essential qualities to have to master speed reading:

- Motivation: Mastering speed reading takes time and effort, so it is crucial to have strong motivation and clear goals. If you have a good reason to improve your reading, you will be more likely to practice the techniques and persevere when it becomes problematic.

- Concentration: Speed reading requires concentration and focus on the text for long periods. If you have trouble concentrating or paying attention, it is essential before learning to speed read.

- Skimming: Skimming involves not reading each word in isolation but skimming the text to get the gist. To do this, you must be able to read diagonally and quickly locate keywords and essential information.

- The ability to process information quickly: Mastering speed reading also involves processing information quickly and putting it into perspective to understand its meaning. If you have trouble processing information quickly, it is essential to work on this skill before you begin learning to speed read.

- Mental Flexibility: Finally, mastering speed reading requires mental flexibility and the ability to adapt quickly to new situations. If you have trouble adjusting to new situations or changing your thinking, working on this skill before you begin learning speed reading is crucial.

Mastering speed reading requires strong motivation, the ability to concentrate, read diagonally, process information quickly, and have mental flexibility. If you work on these qualities and skills, you will be able to master speed reading and enjoy all the benefits it can bring to your learning and success. Remember, it is essential and practice regularly to improve these skills and achieve your speed-reading goals.

There are many techniques and methods for improving these qualities and skills, and you will find many tips and exercises in this book to help you develop them. Take the time to read and practice these tips, and don't hesitate to practice regularly to see real progress in your reading and comprehension. With motivation, focus, skimming ability, mental flexibility, and the ability to process information quickly, you can master speed reading and achieve your speed-reading goals.

Everyone can learn how to read quickly regardless of age, education level, or line of work. It's a prevalent misperception that those with particular abilities or talents are the only ones who can read quickly. But nothing could be further from the truth than this. Anyone may learn and improve their speed reading abilities with commitment and effort.

The traits and abilities needed for rapid reading, such as focus, skimming, and quick information processing, should be noted that they are not prerequisites. Don't give up, even if you believe you now lack specific abilities. Through training and practice, they can be honed and developed. Therefore, fast reading is available to everyone, whether they want to save time on their reading tasks as students, become more productive as professionals, or learn more.

It is obvious what advantages quick reading has. You may save time, learn more, and be more productive by reading more quickly and with higher comprehension. Your personal and professional lives could be significantly affected by this. You can improve your academic performance or professional prospects and free up more time by realizing your full reading ability.

You should be able to reach your full potential as a reader without fear or inexperience. Anyone willing to put time and effort can learn how to read quickly. So take charge of your reading right now and set off on your path to becoming a faster, more effective reader. Your investment in time and knowledge will be more than worthwhile.

CHAPTER 1 : PREREQUISITE

IV. Three prerequisites to improve your understanding

Understanding the connection between reading speed and understanding is crucial. Even though these two skills are closely related, they are still different things that may be learned independently. For readers to become effective, it is essential to comprehend this difference.

Both reading comprehension and speed are crucial abilities that can significantly affect your personal and professional life. You may have an advantage in your education or work if you can rapidly and effectively acquire and comprehend knowledge. However, reading quickly doesn't necessarily imply that you fully comprehend the book. On the other hand, reading slowly while fully understanding the material might be time-consuming and require more time to assimilate substantial amounts of information effectively.

It is crucial to concentrate on both reading comprehension and speed. Faster reading with better comprehension can prevent you from overlooking essential information or misinterpreting the material. It's important to balance speed and understanding because of this. You may improve your reading efficiency and ability to comprehend information rapidly by working on both skills simultaneously.

It's also crucial to remember that these abilities can be acquired over time through training and practice. Therefore, keep in mind that it's always possible to get better if you need assistance with either speed or comprehension. You may improve your reading speed and efficiency to comprehend information more quickly and effectively with commitment and effort.

Pay attention to both abilities and work to increase reading comprehension and speed. By working on both, you may maximize your reading abilities and obtain an advantage in your school or profession. Therefore, strive and practice consistently, and you will reap the rewards of reading in a well-rounded way.

Before we move on to the following chapters on speed reading techniques, it is important to highlight three prerequisites that can significantly increase reading speed and comprehension of texts.

First, lexical poverty can have significant major significance to speed reading. Indeed, if you don't know the meaning of certain words, you will be forced to slow down your reading to understand them or to stop completely to look for their definition. This can down your reading speed and alter your understanding of the text. Working on your vocabulary to read quickly and fully understand the texts you are reading is essential.

Second, reading slowly can positively impact your comprehension. If you read too slowly, you may have difficulty following the argument's flow and remembering details in the text. By increasing your reading speed, you can process more information in less time, allowing you to understand better what you read.

Finally, a lack of interest or motivation can also impact your understanding of texts. If you are not interested in the topic you are reading about, you will tend to lose focus and miss important information. Similarly, if you don't have the motivation to learn or understand the text, you may be less likely to make an effort to read it carefully and memorize it. Finding topics you are passionate about and developing your motivation for reading to maximize your comprehension of the texts is essential.

Lexical poverty

Reading comprehension is a critical skill that allows you to read and understand information. However, there are times when you may need help understanding a text, even if you have a good reading speed. In some cases, these comprehension problems may be due to lexical poverty, i.e., a lack of vocabulary.

Here's how lexical poverty can affect your text comprehension:

1. You may need help understanding the meaning of words: You need to know the importance of a word to understand the importance of the text as a whole.

2. You may have trouble following the author's argument: If you need help understanding the author's words, you may follow their reasoning and understand their ideas.

3. You may need help remembering the content of the text: If you need help understanding the meaning

of words, you will need help placing the content of the text.

Vocabulary is an essential part of our language and our ability to communicate. The more words you have at your disposal, the more accurately and expressively you can share. However, sometimes you may need help finding the right words, or you may need to learn the meaning of certain words. Fortunately, there are many ways to strengthen your vocabulary and become a better communicator. Here are some simple steps to follow:

1. Read regularly: Reading is a great way to learn new words and strengthen your vocabulary. Choose books that interest you and challenge you to discover terms.

2. Do vocabulary exercises: many exercises and games can help you learn and retain new words.

3. Use a dictionary: If you don't know the meaning of a word, look it up in a dictionary. This will help you understand the words' importance and the text better.

4. Talk with people: Talk with people who use a rich and diverse vocabulary. This will help you discover new words and better understand their use.

5. Write regularly: Writing is another great way to use vocabulary. Try to use new words in your writing and look for new ways to say things.

You can significantly improve your reading comprehension by building your vocabulary and practicing reading regularly. Remember, reading comprehension is a skill learned over time and with practice, so keep working and improving.

Insufficient reading speed

Your capacity to understand and remember information from a text can be significantly impacted by the rate you read. It can only be easy to comprehend the overall relevance and meaning of the text you are reading if you read slowly. This might make it more challenging to understand the argument and recognize the crucial details and connections among the concepts, making reading less pleasurable.

Slow reading can have a detrimental effect on comprehension in addition to causing boredom, aggravation, and a lack of desire to read more. These unfavorable feelings can make it harder for you to concentrate and comprehend the text, making it harder to remember what you are reading. Furthermore, reading slowly can make you more stressed since you could feel pressured to keep up with people who read faster or finish material by a specific deadline.

On the other hand, reading at a pace that allows you to keep your attention on the text and comprehend its content can improve your comprehension and memory. You can more readily follow the argument, recognize the main points, and understand the connections between concepts when you read at a comfortable pace. By doing so, you may find reading more enjoyable and be better able to remember what you read.

It's crucial to remember that reading comprehension and speed are distinct abilities that can be developed separately. While reading swiftly can be done without necessarily understanding everything read, reading slowly can also be done while understanding the book completely. These two abilities work together to create a well-rounded reading strategy that allows you to read quickly while yet understanding the text altogether.

It's crucial to practice frequently if you want to increase your reading comprehension and speed. This can entail workouts to sharpen your focus and concentration and strategies like skimming, scanning, and previewing. To avoid weariness, which might impede your reading ability, it is also crucial to take breaks, stretch, and rest your eyes.

Compelling reading depends on both reading speed and comprehension. Working on your comprehension skills can help you ensure that you fully remember the material you read, even though it's crucial to read at a speed that enables you to focus and comprehend the meaning of the text. You can become a more effective and efficient reader by finding a balance between these two talents and frequently practicing, which will help you read faster, more clearly, and more enjoyable.

It is important to note that the ideal reading speed varies from person to person and depends on many factors, such as the individual's comprehension level, the type of text, and the purpose of the reading. However, reading too slowly can generally lead to comprehension and memory problems. Reading too quickly can lead to issues due to needing more time to process and remember information.

Increasing your reading speed allows you to process more information in less time and better understand and retain what you read. Reading faster, you can grasp the text's overall meaning and understand the author's argument better. You will also be able to retain important information from them more easily because your brain will have time to memorize it as you read on.

Lack of interest or motivation

We must underline how important it is to realize that increased reading comprehension cannot be obtained alone by increasing reading speed. One must consider various factors to improve your capacity to understand and retain knowledge.

The effectiveness of your reading abilities is greatly influenced by additional elements, such as keeping a high degree of concentration and focus. Your brain processes and retains information more effectively when fully engrossed in what you are reading. Because of this, it is crucial to keep your interest in the subject and your motivation high.

Interest in the subject can significantly impact your ability to understand and remember information. Your brain is more likely to actively engage with the content when you are reading something you are enthusiastic about, which results in a deeper degree of learning and recall.

Although reading speed plays a significant role in understanding, it is not the sole. To truly advance your reading abilities, it is essential to consider additional factors such as level of focus, drive, and enthusiasm for the subject.

For example, if you are not focused on what you are reading, you will have difficulty retaining information and understanding the text. Similarly, if you don't have motivation or interest in the topic, you may be less likely to read carefully and make an effort to understand important details.

Working on your concentration and motivation to maximize your comprehension of texts is essential. You can, for example, find a quiet, distraction-free environment to read in, set clear and motivating reading goals, or find topics you are passionate about to encourage you to read.

CHAPTER 1 : PREREQUISITE

V. *Eye functioning in reading*

The fovea, located in the center of the macula, is the region of the retina where visual acuity is most acute due to the presence of two types of photoreceptor cells in this area: cones and rods. The cones, primarily sensitive to color and detail, are most effective in bright light. In contrast, the rods, which are especially sensitive to shades of gray and motion, are particularly useful in the dark or at night.

It is important to note that cones represent only 5% of photoreceptors and are mainly concentrated in the fovea, where their density decreases rapidly as they move. On the other hand, Rods represent nearly 95% of photoreceptor cells and have their maximum density in the retina's peripheral retina before decreasing towards the fovea, where they are absent.

It is also important to note that the fovea plays a crucial role in our ability to read and understand quickly. Indeed, when we read, we mainly use our fovea to fix our eyes on the words and sentences we read, which allows us to read faster and better understand what we read.

Therefore, taking care of our fovea and maintaining good visual acuity is essential to fully enjoy all the benefits of speed reading. To do this, it is recommended to protect our eyes from the blue light of screens, to wear sunglasses when we are exposed to sunlight light, and to take regular breaks to relax our eyes when we read or work on a computer.

It is true that the cones, which are more sensitive to details, contribute to a superior visual acuity in the center of our vision, corresponding to the fovea, compared to the periphery of our field of vision. However, this difference in sensitivity is not the only explanation for this superiority of visual acuity in the central zone of the fovea.

Indeed, cones transmit visual information directly to the brain. In contrast, information transmitted by rods is aggregated, i.e., information received by several rods is averaged before being transmitted to the brain by a single ganglion cell. This difference in the transmission of visual communication can also explain the superiority of visual acuity in the fovea compared to the periphery.

This difference in an organization affects the perception of micro-contrast. If one cone receives bright light and its neighbor receives less intense light, the brain will perceive a clear contrast between a band and a dark area. If, on the other hand, two neighboring cones receive the same contrasting light, the brain will only see a gray area, the result of the average between the light and dark spots.

All this information about cones and rods significantly affects how we read. Indeed, texts are made of lines, generally dark on a light background, and being able to distinguish precisely a contrast between a light and a dark area is essential to recognize the visual elements of the writing.

If the light imprint of a word touches the fovea, the cones will easily discern its details and transmit them with excellent fidelity to the brain. If, on the other hand, the word touches the peripheral part of the retina (outside the fovea), it will be transmitted as an average contrast and will appear blurred to our brain. This is why our eyes make movements when we read, to keep the word on the fovea and thus read it accurately. The fovea is, therefore, the area where most of the word recognition is done.

Even if our visual acuity is superior to the fovea, the information transmitted by the peripheral zones of our field of vision needs to be addressed entirely. Numerous studies have shown that peripheral vision allows us to read more efficiently.

For example, peripheral vision allows us to recognize certain words, such as short words and familiar words, before the fovea stops, allowing it to skip them to gain speed. Thus, peripheral vision is helpful for reading, even if it does not allow visual acuity as acute as the fovea.

CHAPTER 2 : BASICS

VI. Speed reading: 10 basics point - avoid common mistakes

Read faster while understanding

When learning speed reading, it is important to understand the purpose of this technique. So what is the purpose of speed reading?

In reality, the purpose of speed reading is twofold. First, the purpose of speed reading is to allow you to read faster. The faster you read, the more you can read in less time. This can help you save time in your daily life, whether you are reading emails, articles, or books.

Second, speed reading aims to help you understand what you are reading. If you read faster but need help understanding what you are reading, you haven't gained anything. So speed reading allows you to read faster while better understanding what you are reading. This will enable you to retain information more effectively and use it more productively.

You must recognize your beginning point, as mastering fast reading starts with a critical evaluation of your existing reading proficiency. This assessment is crucial in figuring out where to concentrate your efforts and how to accelerate your growth.

A reading speed test is one of the best ways to determine your reading pace and comprehension level.

Numerous online reading speed tests are accessible, and they can give you essential information about your reading habits and abilities. These tests are made to gauge how quickly and thoroughly you read, and the results might show you what areas of your reading and comprehension need improvement.

You can more effectively set goals for your speed reading development if you are aware of your starting level. Having a specific objective in mind can help you stay motivated and focused while you work towards your goal, whether to increase your reading speed or enhance your comprehension.

It's also crucial to monitor your development while practicing speed reading. You may see the practical consequences of your hard work and dedication by completing reading speed tests regularly and keeping track of your improvement. This can be inspiring and will encourage you to stick with your aim.

Knowing your starting point is an essential step in developing fast reading skills. You will be better prepared to make significant progress and get the outcomes you want if you take the time to evaluate your present skills and create achievable goals. Take a reading speed test to start your path to becoming a quicker and more effective reader!

It is also essential to consider the type of text you are reading. If you read mostly fiction, your reading speed will be different than reading articles or technical documents. So consider the kind of text you read when evaluating your reading speed.

Knowing your starting level in speed reading will help you progress and achieve your reading goals. So don't hesitate to take a reading speed test and consider the type of text you read to determine your starting level in speed reading. Then you can implement an action plan to improve your speed and reading comprehension.

It is important to note that knowing your starting level in speed reading does not mean you are limited to that level. Instead, it simply gives you a base to work from and allows you to determine your goals for improvement. So be encouraged if your reading speed is lower than you would like. With practice and perseverance, you can improve your speed and comprehension of speed reading.

Reading techniques and breathing.

A good technique is essential for reading quickly and thoroughly understanding what you read. But why is it so important?

First of all, a good reading technique allows you to read faster. If you have an effective reading technique, you can skim through a text quickly and read more words in less time. This can help you save time in your daily life and enjoy your reading more.

Second, a good reading technique helps you understand what you are reading. If you have an ineffective reading technique, you may need to fully understand what you are reading and lose track of the story. With an effective reading technique, you will better understand the text's overall meaning and retain the information more effectively.

Finally, a good reading technique allows you to read more comfortably and enjoyably. If you have an ineffective reading technique, you may get tired more quickly and become discouraged.

With an effective reading technique, you can read more comfortably and enjoyably, allowing you to get the most out of your reading.

In summary, the importance of good reading techniques must be considered. It allows you to read faster, to understand better what you are reading, and to read more comfortably and enjoyably. So if you want to improve your reading speed and comprehension, don't hesitate to work on your reading technique. It can make all the difference!

It is important to note that each person has a unique reading technique, and there may be many ways to improve your reading technique. So, be encouraged if you need help finding a method that works for you. Take the time to experiment and see what works best for you. By practicing different reading techniques and doing regular practice, you should be able to develop an effective reading technique that will allow you to read faster and better understand what you are reading.

To develop your reading speed, working on your reading technique is crucial. But what should you consider when working on your reading technique?

First, it is important to work on your eye fixation. Your eyes should move over the text smoothly and at a constant speed. If your eyes dwell on a letter or word for a short time, it can slow down your reading speed. You can use a finger or stylus to follow the text or a reading line to improve your eye fixation.

Next, it is vital to work on keyword recognition. If you can quickly recognize keywords in a text, you will be able to understand the overall meaning of the text better and read faster. You can use memorization techniques to improve your keyword recognition, such as creating mental maps or writing summaries.

Finally, it is crucial to work on your breathing when you read. If you hold your breath or breathe erratically, it can affect your concentration and reading speed. Try to breathe evenly and profoundly to improve your reading speed.

The different types of reading: choose the right one for the situation

There are several types of reading, and it is important to know which ones to use depending on the situation. But what are these different types of reading, and how can you use them effectively?

First, there is linear reading. Linear reading involves reading a text sequentially, starting at the beginning and ending at the end. This is the most common type of reading and is ideal when you want to understand the general meaning of a text and retain the information in detail.

Then there is skimming. Skimming is reading a text quickly to get the gist and find critical information. It is helpful when you need more time to read a whole text or when you want to locate important information quickly.

Finally, there is scanning. Scanning is the process of quickly skimming a text to find specific information.

This is a valuable type of reading when you need to find a particular piece of information in a text quickly and you only have time to read part of the text.

There are several types of reading, and it is important to choose the right style for the situation. Linear reading is ideal for understanding the general meaning of a text and retaining information in detail. Skimming is useful when you want to locate important information in a text quickly. Scanning reading is useful when finding specific information in a text quickly.

Therefore, choosing the right type of reading according to the situation is vital to read effectively. But why is it so important to choose the right kind of reading?

First, choosing the right type of reading will save you time. If you use the right type of reading, you will be able to read faster and find the information you are looking for more easily. This can help you save time in your daily life and enjoy your reading more.

Second, choosing the right type of reading helps you better understand and retain the information. If you use the correct type of reading, you may need to fully understand what you are reading or retain the information effectively. By choosing the right kind of reading, you can better understand and retain the information in the texts you read.

Finally, choosing the right type of reading material allows you to read more comfortably and enjoyably. If you use the wrong type of reading material, you may get tired more quickly and become discouraged. Choosing the suitable reading material allows you to read more comfortably and enjoyably, enabling you to get the most out of your reading.

Linear reading is the most common type of reading and is ideal for understanding the general meaning of a text and retaining information in detail. However, there are some situations in which there are better options than linear reading. But what are these situations, and why is linear reading not always appropriate?

There are situations in which you need more time to read an entire text. If you have a busy schedule and need to scan much text, linear reading may need to be faster and more efficient. In this case, it is better to use a faster type of reading, such as skimming or scanning.

Then there are situations in which you need to find specific information in a text quickly. If you are looking for a particular piece of information in a text and need more time to read the entire text, linear reading may need to be faster and more efficient. In this case, it is better to use a faster type of reading, such as scanning, which allows you to scan a text to find specific information quickly.

Finally, there are situations where you only need to understand or retain some of the details of a text. If you are reading a text to get the gist and locate key information, linear reading can be unnecessarily slow and detailed. In this case, it is better to use a faster type of reading, such as skimming, which allows you to quickly read a text to understand the gist and locate key information.

So there are some situations with better options than linear reading. If you don't have time to read a whole text, if you need to find a specific piece of information in a text quickly, or if you don't need to understand or retain all the details of a text, it's best to use a faster type of reading.

In summary, choosing suitable reading material is essential for effective reading. It saves time, helps you understand and retain information better, and makes reading more comfortable and enjoyable. So, when you read, remember to choose the right type of reading for the situation to get the maximum benefit. By using these different types of reading effectively, you should better understand and retain the information in the texts you read.

Improve your understanding: visualization and memorization techniques.

Implementing visualization and memorization techniques is important to improve your understanding of what you read. But how can you use these techniques effectively?

First, you can use the technique of creating mental maps. But what is mind mapping, and how can it help you better understand and retain information?

Creating mental maps is the process of graphically representing the information in a text through diagrams or schematics. This allows you to visualize the organization of the information and understand how all the ideas are related. For example, if you are reading a text about the history of France, you can create a mental map representing the critical events in the history of France and how they relate to each other.

By creating mental maps, you can better understand the information organization in a text and how all the ideas are related. This allows you to better understand and retain the information in the texts you read.

Next, you can use the technique of summary writing. Summary writing involves summarizing the information in a text concisely and accurately. This allows you to understand better and remember the gist of what you have read. For example, if you read a text about different types of clouds, you can write a summary of that text with the main types of clouds and their characteristics.

When writing a summary, you should be able to select the most important information and present it concisely and accurately. This allows you to understand better the essence of what you have read and to remember it more easily.

Finally, you can use the repetition technique. Repetition means repeating aloud or mentally the information you have read. This allows you to fix the information in your memory and retain it better. For example, if you read a text about the names of plants, you can repeat the names of the plants mentally or aloud to help you remember them.

By repeating the information you have read, you fix the information in your memory and are better able to retain it.

The repetition technique involves repeating aloud or mentally the information you have read. This technique is simple and easy to implement but can be less effective than the "active recall" method. By repeating the information you have read, you are not checking whether you have understood it, and you need to work on understanding the information.

On the other hand, the active recall involves answering questions or reciting the information you have read. This technique is more effective than repetition because it allows you to check your understanding of the information and work on your comprehension. By answering questions or actively reciting the information you have read, you are forced to think about it and relate it to what you already know.

To use the "active recall" method in speed reading, here are some steps to follow:

1. Select the most important information from the text you are reading. This allows you to target the most relevant information and focus on it.

2. Formulate questions about the information you have selected. For example, if you are reading a text about the history of France, you can ask questions like "When was the French Republic proclaimed?", "Who was the first president of the French Republic?"

3. Answer the questions you have formulated. This allows you to actively recite the information you have read and check for understanding.

4. Repeat the exercise several times to fix the information in your memory. The more you repeat the exercise, the more you will be able to retain the information permanently.

Focus and distraction: stay focused on your reading

Have you ever found yourself reading a text without really understanding its content? You may have been distracted by your phone, work environment, or other external elements. To better understand and retain the information you are reading, it is crucial to focus on what you are reading and not be distracted by external factors.

You may be used to reading while multitasking, that is while doing several tasks at the same time. For example, you may read a text while watching TV or listening to music. However, multitasking can be counterproductive, as it prevents you from focusing on what you are reading and better understanding the information.

To avoid being distracted by external elements, here are some tips for implementing:

1. Create a quiet and pleasant work environment. If you are constantly distracted by noise or elements in your work environment, creating a peaceful, pleasant workspace to focus on what you are reading is vital.

2. Unplug your phone or put it on "do not disturb" mode while you read. This will allow you to concentrate without being interrupted by notifications or calls.

3. Use a distraction-blocking application, such as Freedom or Cold Turkey, to block access to certain websites or applications that may distract you while you read.

4. Take regular breaks to relax and refocus. Taking time to relax and refocus can help you concentrate better when you return to your reading.

5. Make a priority list and plan your reading time. If you need help focusing on what you are reading, it can be helpful to plan your reading time and prioritize the texts you need to read. This will help you focus on what is most important and be focused on more urgent tasks. Here's a technique you can use to focus in 5 minutes:

1. Find a nice, quiet place to sit or lie down. Avoid sitting in a noisy or bright place.

2. Close your eyes and take several deep breaths. Try to relax and refocus on your breathing.

3. Do a small meditation exercise. You can imagine a peaceful landscape or focus on a mantra or a positive phrase. This will help you calm down and refocus.

4. Open your eyes and look at an object in the distance. It could be a tree, a cloud, or any other object. Try to focus on this object for a few minutes.

5. Return to your current reading or task. Try to focus on your actions and not be distracted by external elements.

6. By implementing this technique, you should be better able to focus and understand what you are reading or doing.

Speed reading: don't push too hard at first

When you first start using the speed reading technique, it is tempting to want to read as fast as possible to achieve better results. However, it is important to read slowly at first, as this can be discouraging and affect your comprehension.

Reading too fast can leave you needing to understand all the information in the text and feeling frustrated.

This can discourage you from continuing your speed reading practice.

It is, therefore, important to start slowly and work your way up to improve your reading speed. By increasing your reading speed gradually, you will be better able to understand and retain what you read.

Setting reasonable goals and trying to reach a high reading speed slowly is also essential. Speed reading takes practice and patience, and it is normal not to achieve dramatic results on the first attempt.

Therefore, you shouldn't get discouraged and persevere in your speed reading practice. By practicing regularly and setting reasonable goals, you will be able to improve your reading speed and achieve better results sustainably.

Speed reading is just one tool to improve your comprehension and recall of what you read. It is, therefore, essential to focus on something other than your reading speed and to pay attention to other reading techniques, such as creating mental maps or writing summaries, which can also help you better understand and retain what you read.

You must set reasonable and achievable goals when using the speed reading technique. For example, you can set a goal to increase your reading speed by 10% each week or to read a book of X pages in X hours.

These goals also need to be specific and measurable, so you can assess your progress and know where you stand. For example, you can set a goal to read a 300-page book in 3 hours and use a stopwatch to measure your reading time and ensure you're meeting your goal. Then repeat that goal in 3 months in less time.

Set goals that motivate you to persevere in your speed reading practice. For example, you can set a goal to read a book from your reading list using the speed reading technique or to read a book for work or leisure using speed reading.

Improve your reading comprehension and speed: read aloud.

Reading aloud can be an effective way to improve your reading comprehension and speed. By reading aloud, you are forced to focus more on the text and read more slowly, which can help you better understand what you are reading.

In addition, by reading aloud, you can hear the words and phrases you are having trouble with and dwell on them to better understand them. This can be especially helpful if you need help understanding certain parts of the text or if you come across words you need to learn.

Finally, reading aloud can help you develop your pronunciation and diction, which can benefit your overall communication.

It is important to note that reading aloud is not a speed reading technique but a complementary technique that can help you improve your comprehension and reading speed. Therefore, it is important to allow yourself to read aloud and continue working on other aspects of speed reading, such as eye fixation, keyword recognition, and breathing.

Also, it is important not to read aloud in a monotonous or boring way, as this can demotivate and discourage you from reading. Try to vary your intonation and rhythm to make your reading more enjoyable and engaging.

Finally, finding the right balance between reading aloud and silently is vital. Try to read aloud regularly, but only sometimes, so that you don't get used to it and continue to develop your silent reading skills.

Silent reading is reading in your head without saying the words out loud. Subvocalization, on the other hand, consists of mentally pronouncing the words you read in your head.

Silent reading is generally considered more effective than subvocalization because it allows you to read faster. Subvocalization can slow down your reading speed because it requires you to pronounce each word you read mentally.

It is important to note that subvocalization is a natural mechanism that can help you understand and remember what you read. However, it is possible to reduce subvocalization by practicing silent reading and working on your reading technique.

To reduce subvocalization and improve your reading speed, there are several techniques you can try:

- Use fingers or markers to follow the lines of text to avoid mentally pronouncing each word.

- Use a voice reader, such as a text-to-speech application, which will allow you to read faster without having to pronounce each word mentally.

- Practice silent reading, which means reading in your head without saying the words out loud.

- Work on your reading technique in general, such as eye fixation and keyword recognition.

It is important to note that reducing subvocalization is challenging to master and requires training and practice. It is, therefore, essential to persevere and continue to work on this aspect of speed reading to see long-term results.

Take breaks for better retention.

Taking regular breaks is essential to maintaining your concentration and comprehension when you read. It allows you to rest your eyes and mind and retain what you read better.

It is recommended that you take a break every 20-30 minutes of reading, depending on your reading pace and fatigue level. During these breaks, you can close your eyes and relax for a few minutes or walk and stretch to relax your muscles.

It is also essential to vary your activity during your breaks. For example, you can do a little sport, meditate, or chat with a friend or colleague. This will help you stay focused and retain what you have read better.

In summary, regular breaks are essential to maintain concentration and reading comprehension. Don't hesitate to vary your activities during these breaks to stay focused and retain what you have read better.

Sleep is also one of the critical elements of memory and learning. During sleep, our brains sort and store the information we have acquired during the day, which allows us to retain it better.

Studies show that sleep plays a vital role in consolidating long-term memory. During sleep, our brains review information learned during the day and strengthened neural links, allowing us to remember it better.

Therefore, getting enough sleep is essential to allow our brains to work efficiently and retain what we have read or learned better. According to experts, it is recommended to sleep between 7 and 9 hours per night to be fit and healthy. I

Four texts to practice speed reading

To improve your speed reading skills, four practice texts will help you develop your reading speed while maintaining good comprehension. Whether you're a beginner or want more practice, these texts are suitable for all levels and will provide a stimulating challenge. Start with the first text and work your way up to the last to see your progress and reach new reading speed goals. Remember to take the time to understand what you are reading, as this is the main objective of speed reading. Have a good workout!

To calculate the reading speed of a text, you can use the following formula: Reading speed (words per minute) = number of words/reading time (in minutes)

For example, if you read the first 305-word text in 7 minutes, your reading speed would be Reading speed (words per minute) = 305 words / 7 minutes = 43,57 words per minute.

TEXT 1: 366 words

Philosophers, scientists, and everyday people have all been fascinated by the topic of time for ages. We all have a finite amount of it, but it is an endlessly intriguing idea. Managing our time successfully is crucial because every moment is valuable and cannot be retrieved after it has passed. The adage "time is money" refers to this situation, although, in actuality, time is significantly more valuable than money. Time cannot be made up, but money can be made, spent, and even lost.

Using time management strategies such as speed reading is one of them. One can read more quickly using eye movement and information-processing techniques while still understanding what they are reading. People who need to read content quickly and have busy schedules may find this strategy especially helpful.

You can use a few techniques to hone your speed-reading abilities. The first is by doing particular activities developed to boost reading speed. For instance, you can aim to finish reading little texts in a predetermined amount of time or read lengthy materials quickly via word skimming. There are other software tools for speed reading training that offer workouts and keep tabs on your progress.

Regular reading is the second method for developing speed reading. As you read more, you'll feel more at ease with the practice and be able to pick up reading speed more quickly. Additionally, picking books that interest you will help you stay motivated and concentrated.

It is crucial to remember that reading comprehension shouldn't be sacrificed for quick reading. The method is only helpful if you read slowly and need help understanding the content. It is advisable to read slowly and carefully, and be bold and go over some passages again if you need to. You may improve your speed reading abilities and become more effective in your daily life with time, patience, and practice.

In conclusion, time is a precious resource that shouldn't be ignored. Striking a balance between speed and comprehension is crucial when using speed reading as a strategy for time management. You can enhance your speed reading abilities and make the most of the little time we have in life by practicing frequently and exercising patience.

TEXT 2: 293 words

Memory is an essential cognitive function that allows us to store and recall information. It is divided into two parts: short-term memory and long-term memory. Short-term memory is like a buffer that allows us to temporarily store information before transferring it to long-term memory. Long-term memory is like a hard drive that holds information permanently.

Speed reading can be an effective way to strengthen your memory. By reading quickly, you force your brain to process information faster, which can improve your ability to remember. However, reading at a reasonable speed is important at the expense of comprehension. You need to understand what you're reading to remember it effectively.

There are several ways to strengthen your memory using speed reading. The first is to read regularly. The more you read, the more your brain will be trained to process and remember information quickly. You can also read texts that interest you, as you will then be more motivated and focused.

Another way to strengthen your memory is to review what you have read regularly. This can be done by rereading the text, making review cards, or discussing the content with someone else. This can help you remember and retain the information in the long run.

Finally, taking care of your mental and physical health is essential. A healthy diet, regular exercise, and good stress management can all help improve your memory. Feel free to take time to relax and unwind so that your brain can function effectively.

In summary, speed reading can be an effective way to strengthen your memory as long as you don't neglect comprehension and take care of your mental and physical health. With practice and patience, you should be able to develop your speed reading skills and strengthen your memory.

TEXT 3: 508 words

I need to figure out where to start. I was taken by surprise. I didn't expect our relationship to end the way it did. We had been together for over two years, and everything seemed to be going well. We had our ups and downs like any couple, but I was convinced we were meant to be together.

Then one day, she told me she needed to take time for herself. She said she didn't know what she wanted and needed time away from me to think about it. I was caught off guard. I didn't expect that at all. I tried to convince her to stay, but she was firm. She said she needed time and needed to know how long it would take.

I was devastated. I didn't know what to do. I tried to show her how much I loved her and how much I wanted her to stay, but she was determined to leave. I finally accepted her decision, even though it broke my heart. I tried to give her space and respect her need for time, but it was hard. I couldn't stop thinking about her and wondering what was going on.

In the end, she never came back. She told me that she had made up her mind and didn't want to be with me anymore. I was utterly devastated. I couldn't believe that our relationship was over. I tried to convince her to change her mind, but she was determined. I finally accepted the reality and started trying to move on.

It was one of the worst experiences of my life. I will never forget how I felt when I discovered that the person I had shared so much with no longer wanted to be with me. I'm still trying to figure out what happened. We had our ups and downs like any couple, but I believed we would get through all our problems together. I was caught off guard by her decision to leave and had a hard time accepting it. I tried to show her how much I loved her and how much I wanted her to stay, but she was firm.

I went through all kinds of emotions during this difficult time. I felt sadness, anger, disappointment, and disbelief. I found it hard to believe that our relationship was over, and I spent much time trying to figure out what had happened. Eventually, I came to terms with reality and began to try to move on, although it was difficult.

I can't say I'm entirely over that breakup. It's something that will stay with me forever. But I have learned much from this experience and have grown as a man. I learned to be stronger and not let my heart be broken in this way in the future. I also learned the importance of communicating openly and honestly in a relationship and not being afraid to say what I feel. This experience was painful, but I ended up learning valuable lessons that will serve me throughout my life.

TEXT 4: 270 words

The space expedition is one of the most daring challenges humanity has ever faced. Since man first set foot on the Moon in 1969, we have made countless advances in space exploration. We have sent probes into the solar system, built space stations to house astronauts in orbit, and even sent rovers to Mars.

But space exploration also brings many challenges and dangers. Astronauts who go on missions must deal with extreme conditions, such as the vacuum of space, solar storms, and cosmic radiation. They also have to deal with mental strain and stress, as they are often cut off from the world for long periods.

Despite these challenges, space expedition remains an exciting and fascinating field. It allows us to discover new things about our planet and the universe around us. It also offers us new perspectives on life and humanity's possible possibilities.

Space expedition is also a constantly evolving field. We recently launched the first crewed mission to Mars and have many projects underway to explore other parts of the universe. We have also developed new technologies, such as reusable rockets and autonomous space vehicles, to make space missions safer and more efficient.

In summary, space exploration is a fascinating and exciting field that allows us to discover new things about our universe and planet. Despite the challenges and dangers, we have made many advances in space exploration and have many projects underway to continue exploring the universe. We have also developed new technologies to make space missions safer and more efficient. Space expedition is an ever-evolving field, and I look forward to seeing what the future holds.

CHAPTER 2 : BASICS

VII. Improve your reading speed by working on your technique

It is important to emphasize that the ten points discussed above have undeniable theoretical value and are essential to your learning speed reading. They provide the foundation for building your mastery of this skill.

However, it is also crucial to practice more advanced techniques that will allow you to speed up your reading while maintaining a high level of comprehension. Although this list is not exhaustive, I will present here the ones that have helped me personally, as well as the ones that have proven to be effective for the people I have had the opportunity to accompany in their progress in speed reading.

Hover and scan

Scanning is a fast-reading technique that allows you to quickly process a large amount of information in a short time. This technique consists of quickly skimming a text to get an overview, then scanning the most crucial information for a deeper understanding.

Scanning is beneficial for quickly reading long, complex texts, such as research articles or technical books. It allows you to process information quickly to understand the text's essence and orient yourself within it.

Using the Hover and Scan technique, you can improve your reading speed and comprehension of text. This technique can help you process information better and make better decisions faster. If you want to improve your reading speed and understanding of texts, the Hover and Scan technique is one to try.

The fast flyover

Skimming is a quick reading technique that allows you to quickly process a large amount of information in a short period. This technique will enable you to get an overview of a text and to orient yourself in it. It is beneficial when you need to understand the gist of a text without having to read every word.

There are several hovering techniques you can use depending on your reading goals. Here are some examples of hovering methods:

The read-aloud technique: This technique consists of reading aloud, removing unnecessary words, and emphasizing keywords. It allows you to process information and orient yourself in the text quickly.

The diagonal skimming technique: This technique consists of quickly reading the top lines from left to right, then the bottom lines from right to left, and so on. It allows you to process information and orient yourself in the text quickly.

Skimming by rule: This technique consists of quickly reading each line by following a rule (for example, by following a finger or a stylus) and removing unnecessary words. It allows you to process information and orient yourself in the text quickly.

Using the hover technique, you can quickly process information and orient yourself in a text. Feel free to try different hovering techniques to find the one that works best for you.

The scan

Speed scanning is a reading technique that aims to increase reading speed while maintaining good comprehension. It consists of "hunting" for important information in a text using a speed reading technique.

To use this technique, knowing what you are looking for is important before you start reading. This allows you to focus on vital information to achieve that goal. It is also essential to familiarize yourself with the content of the text before you start reading to know where to look for important information.

Several scanning techniques for speed reading, such as "slit" or "zone" reading. Slit" reading involves using the eyes to "scan" the text using wide horizontal slits covering several lines simultaneously. Zone reading uses the eyes more vertically, reading groups of words rather than whole lines.

It is important to note that speed scanning is not suitable for all types of text. It is beneficial for reading informational or fictional documents but may be less ideal for reading technical or scientific papers that require attention to detail.

Here are five steps to set up a speed scan:

1. Determine what you are looking for: Before you start reading, it is essential to know what you are looking for in the text. This can be a general idea, a specific concept, or information. This will allow you to focus on vital information to achieve your goal.

2. Familiarize yourself with the text: Before you start reading, skim and familiarize yourself with its contents. Look at the headings, subheadings, and keywords to understand what is in each section. This will help you know where to look for important information.

3. Choose a speed reading technique: There are several speed reading techniques, such as "slit" or "zone" reading. Choose the one that suits you best and allows you to read quickly while understanding the content of the text.

4. Start reading: Once you have determined what you are looking for and have chosen a speed reading technique, start reading the text. Use your speed reading technique to "hunt" for important information and explore new ideas.

5. Take notes: As you read, take notes on what you have read. This will help you better understand and remember the content of the text. You can also use these notes to review later.

In summary:

- Start with a quick skim of the text to get an overview and orient yourself to the text. You can use skimming techniques such as reading diagonally or reading aloud to process information quickly.

- Identify the most critical information and focus on it when scanning. You can use scanning techniques such as dual view or rule reading to process this information more thoroughly.

- Take notes during the scan to help you retain information better. You can use note-taking techniques such as mind mapping or concept mapping to organize your ideas clearly and concisely.

- Practice the Hover and Scan technique regularly to improve your reading speed and comprehension of text. Practice is essential to improve your reading speed and ability to process information quickly. Take the time to regularly read and practice the Hover and Scan technique to enhance reading speed and comprehension.

- Adapt your skimming and scanning technique according to your reading objective. If you need to understand the whole text, you may need to spend more time scanning the information. If you are looking for an overview of the text, you may need to spend less time scanning the information.

Improve speed reading

Improving linear reading in speed reading can be very useful for several reasons.

First of all, linear reading in speed reading can help improve comprehension of the text. When you read linearly, you follow the flow of the text consistently, which enables you to understand the flow of ideas and retain the content of the text better.

Second, linear speed reading can be helpful for quickly finding specific information in a text. When you read linearly, you can use speed reading techniques to "hunt" for important news and explore new ideas. This allows you to quickly find the information you are looking for without going through the entire text.

Finally, linear reading in speed reading can be helpful to retain better and use the information you have read. When you read linearly, you can take notes and make summaries to help you better understand and remember the content of the text. You can also use these notes to review later and apply your learned information.

Find fixing points

The fixation points in speed reading are points on which the eyes rest during reading. They play an essential role in reading speed and text comprehension.

Several factors can influence the fixation points in rapid reading. First, the reading technique used can affect fixation points. For example, the "slit" reading technique involves using wide horizontal slits to cover several lines simultaneously, which can result in broader fixation points. In contrast, the "zone" reading technique uses more minor fixation points to read groups of words rather than whole lines.

Second, the content of the text can influence the fixation points. For example, if the text is dense and complex, the fixation points may be smaller to allow for better understanding.

Finally, the reader's familiarity with the text can influence fixation points. If the reader is familiar with the content of the text, he may have more significant fixation points because he already has a good understanding of the information. On the other hand, if the reader is not familiar with the text content, they may have more minor fixation points to understand the information better.

It is important to note that fixation points in speed reading can vary depending on the individual and the situation. No "ideal" fixation point size will work for all readers in all conditions.

However, by working on your reading technique and taking into account the content and familiarity level of the text, you can adjust your fixation points to improve your reading speed and comprehension.

It is also difficult to give a precise number of fixation points on average because they can vary depending on several factors, such as the reading technique used, the content of the text, and the reader's level of familiarity with the text.

It is estimated that the number of fixation points in rapid reading can vary from 10 to 20 per minute. However, this number may be higher or lower depending on the situation. For example, if you are reading dense, complex text, you may need more fixation points to understand the information better. On the other hand, if you are familiar with the content of the text, you may need fewer fixation points because you already have a good understanding of the information.

The number of fixation points is not necessarily an indicator of reading quality. Some readers may have a higher number of fixation points but better text comprehension, while others may have a lower number of fixation points but worse comprehension. The important thing is to find a reading technique that works for you and allows you to read effectively and understand the content of the text.

Expand the field of vision.

When you read, your visual field is the area of your vision that covers the text you are reading. The narrower your field of vision, the more time you need to scan the text, and the more likely you will make mistakes or miss important information. By widening your field of vision, you can cover more words at a time and improve your reading speed while maintaining a good understanding of the text.

It is important to note that expanding the visual field in speed reading takes practice and practice. You can start with simple exercises to help you become familiar with the technique and develop your visual field. With practice, you should be able to significantly widen your field of vision and improve your reading speed while maintaining a good understanding of the text.

Here are four exercises that can help you expand your visual field in speed reading:

- Slot" exercise: This exercise involves reading lines of words using wide horizontal slots. To begin, place your index finger on the first line of words and move it horizontally to cover several words simultaneously. Drag your index finger to the following line and repeat until you've covered the entire text. You can adjust the width of the slot to suit your comfort level and reading speed.

- Zone" exercise: This exercise involves reading groups of words using more minor fixation points. To begin, place your index finger on the first group of words and move it from left to right to cover each word individually. Drag your index finger to the next group of words and repeat until you've covered the entire text. You can adjust the size of the word groups to suit your comfort level and reading speed.

- "Vertical Slots" exercise: this exercise involves reading columns of words using large vertical slots. To begin, place your index finger on the first column of words and move it vertically to cover several words simultaneously. Drag your index finger to the next column and repeat until you've covered all the text. You can adjust the width of the slot to suit your comfort level and reading speed.

- Scanning" exercise: This exercise consists of quickly scanning the text using a single point of fixation. To begin, place your index finger on the first line of words and move it horizontally to cover each word individually. Drag your index finger to the following line and repeat until you have covered the entire text. You can adjust the movement speed to suit your comfort level and reading speed.

Train your eyes

It is crucial to understand how your eye movements work when reading. Your eyes move erratically, stopping on some words and ignoring others. If you can reduce the number of movements you make per line, you will be able to read much faster. However, it would be best if you were careful because there is a limit to the number of words you can perceive at one time.

According to some studies, you can read eight letters on the right of your eye position but only four on the left, which is about two to three words each time. In addition, you may notice between nine and fifteen spaces on the right, but you can't read them. Regular readers also do not process words on other lines.

To practice, try skipping lines while understanding what you are reading. This should be relatively easy once you get the hang of it.

To improve your reading speed, it is essential to practice reducing the number of eye movements. This is because your brain usually determines where to direct your eyes based on the length or familiarity of the next word. If you can get your eyes used to move accurately across the page, you will be able to read faster.

Here's a simple exercise that will help you practice:

- Place your bookmark on a line of text.

- Draw an X on the bookmark, just above the first word.

- Draw another X on the same line, placing it three words away for easy comprehension, five words out for intermediate-level text, and seven words away for more challenging text.

- Continue to draw X's spaced out in the same way until the end of the line.

- Read quickly by sliding the bookmark down, focusing your eyes only under each X.

This exercise will allow you to train yourself to reduce your eye movements and focus on specific words, which will help you read faster while maintaining good comprehension.

One of the things that can slow down your reading speed the most are regressions and backspaces. Indeed, these actions can save time, so it is essential to avoid them to improve your reading speed.

But what exactly is regression? It is the act of rereading words or sentences you have already read. This usually happens when you think you still need to retain or understand what you've just read. However, it is essential to note that your brain has most likely retained the information, even if you feel otherwise.

To eliminate regressions, it is essential to practice not going back even if you think you have yet to understand the text. Continue reading and let your eyes move forward. Here's an exercise to help you practice:

1. Take a medium-level text and place your bookmark on the first line.

2. Begin reading by letting your eyes glide over each line without looking back.

3. If you need help understanding a word or sentence, don't go back and re-read it. Just continue reading and let your brain integrate the information as you go.

4. Repeat this exercise until you can read the text without returning.

You can read much faster by practicing eliminating regressions and backtracking while maintaining comprehension.

Trusting your brain

It is important to trust your brain for comprehension in speed reading. Our brains can process large amounts of information quickly and efficiently, which allows us to read quickly while maintaining a good understanding of the text.

Relaxing and focusing on the text is essential to trust your brain in speed reading. By using a speed reading technique that suits your reading style and taking the time to familiarize yourself with the content of the text before you start reading, you can help your brain better understand the information.

It is also important not to worry if you don't understand all the information immediately. Our brains can memorize and process large amounts of data, even if we don't understand it immediately.

It is also essential to review and memorize the information you read. By repeating the content of the text aloud or writing a summary, you can help your brain better remember the information and retain it in the long term.

In summary, trusting your brain in speed reading is essential for adequate text comprehension. By using a speed reading technique appropriate for your reading style, taking the time to familiarize yourself with the content of the text, and reviewing and memorizing the information read, you can help your brain better understand and retain the information read quickly and effectively.

Note-taking technique

Taking notes while speed reading can be very helpful in improving comprehension and retention of the text you read. Taking notes throughout the reading can help your brain better process and retain the information in the long term.

There are several ways to take notes in speed reading, such as traditional note-taking, the Cornell method, and note-taking using diagrams and charts. Each method has advantages and disadvantages, and it is vital to find the one that best suits your reading style and needs.

Rapid reading note-taking can also be helpful to help you clarify your ideas and structure your thinking. By summarizing the text you read and rephrasing it in your own way, you can better understand the content and apply it to your life or work.

Many methods of note-taking are considered the best according to scientific studies. According to research, the most appropriate note-taking method depends on several factors, such as the individual's reading style, the text's complexity, and the reading's context.

However, some studies have shown that note-taking using diagrams and charts may be more effective for some people because it allows them to visualize concepts more clearly and better understand the structure of the text. Other studies have shown that note-taking using the Cornell method, which involves dividing the page into two columns and taking notes using short sentences and keywords, may be more effective for some people because it helps to structure the information more clearly.

It is important to note that the best note-taking method depends on your preferences and reading style. It may be helpful to test different note-taking ways and find the one that best suits your reading style and needs.

It is also important to note that speed-reading note-taking is only necessary for some and may not be the best approach for all text types. According to some studies, note-taking may even reduce attention and comprehension for some individuals.

Therefore, finding an approach that suits your reading style and needs is crucial. If you take notes in speed reading, it's important to focus only a little on taking notes and ensure you understand the text before moving on to the next page.

CHAPTER 3 : NEXT LEVEL

VIII. Optimize your reading speed according to the medium: paper or digital

Speed reading is an essential skill that can be developed and improved, regardless of the medium used. But how do you choose between reading on paper and digital media?

According to research, reading on paper can be more enjoyable for some readers because it allows them to detach from the screen and focus better on the text. It can also be easier for some readers because it will enable them to control their reading speed better and not be distracted by notifications or external links. According to some studies, reading on paper can even help with better comprehension and memorization of text, especially for long or complex texts.

Therefore, reading on paper may be preferable for some documents requiring much attention and understanding. For example, if you need to read professional or academic documents, such as reports, research articles, manuals, or textbooks, reading on paper can help you better understand and remember the content. Reading on paper is also preferable if you must prepare for exams or tests, as it helps you better understand and remember the material.

However, reading on digital media may be more convenient for some readers because it allows easy access to additional information through external links. It may also be easier for some readers because it will enable them to control their reading speed and highlight or mark important passages.

Therefore, digital reading is preferable for some materials requiring much practice and quick comprehension. For example, digital reading might be preferable if you read news or articles online because it can help you read quickly and access additional information efficiently. Digital reading is also preferable if you need to quickly understand a large volume of information, such as emails or business documents.

However, it is essential to note that digital reading may be less enjoyable for some readers because it can be more tiring on the eyes and more distracting due to notifications and external links.

According to some studies, reading in digital media may even be less effective for comprehension and memorization of text, especially for long or complex texts.

Therefore, finding a medium that suits your preferences and needs is essential. If you prefer reading on paper and need to understand better and memorize the content of a document, reading on paper may be preferable. If you choose digital reading and need to read quickly and understand a large volume of information quickly, digital reading may be better.

Ultimately, the best way to choose between reading on paper and reading on digital media depends on your preferences and needs.

CHAPTER 3 : NEXT LEVEL

IX. *Speed Reading and Decision Making*

Reading speed, a critical factor in decision making

Reading speed is a crucial element in decision-making. When you are faced with a situation that requires quick decision-making, your reading speed can be critical in allowing you to process all the available information and make an informed decision.

Reading speed is a crucial part of our daily lives, allowing us to quickly process and understand large amounts of information. It also plays an essential role in decision-making, allowing us to react promptly and effectively to situations that come our way. The faster you can read and understand information, the more time you have to think and decide.

However, it is essential to note that reading speed can influence the quality of our decisions. If you read too slowly, you may miss important information or not have time to consider the consequences of your decision entirely. Reading faster can process more information and make more informed decisions.

In addition, reading speed can help us react more quickly to situations that come our way. If you can read and understand the information presented to you quickly

Here are some examples of situations where reading speed may be critical:

- Emergencies: When an emergency arises, it is crucial to make a quick decision to act effectively and protect your safety or the safety of those around you. If you can read and understand relevant information quickly, you can make a decision more quickly and react more effectively.

- Work situations: In a work environment, reading speed can be an asset for making quick decisions and processing information efficiently. For example, if you are a manager and need to make a quick decision based on a report from your team, your reading speed can help you quickly understand the issues and make an informed decision.

- Leisure situations: Even in leisure situations, reading speed can be an asset in making quick decisions. For example, if you are reading a book and need to decide whether or not to continue reading, your reading speed can help you quickly understand the plot and decide whether or not you want to continue.

Reading speed is a crucial component of decision-making. When you are faced with a situation requiring quick decision-making, your reading speed can be critical in allowing you to process all available information and make an informed decision. Reading speed can help you make decisions faster and more efficiently in emergencies, work, or play situations.

Improve your decision-making with speed reading.

Reading speed can play an essential role in everyday decision-making. By using speed reading, you can process more information in less time, making better decisions more quickly and efficiently.

Here are some examples of when you can use speed reading to make better decisions in your daily life:

1. Choosing a book to read: If you're having trouble deciding which book to read, you can use Speed Reading to quickly read summaries and reviews of different books to help you make a choice.

2. Decide where to vacation: If you need help determining where to go on vacation, you can use the Quick Read to quickly read the pros and cons of each destination and make a decision faster.

3. Choosing your next job: If you're looking for a new job, you can use Speed Reading to quickly read

through job postings and job descriptions to promptly find the ones that best match your skills and career goals.

Speed reading can be beneficial in making better decisions in your daily life, allowing you to process more information in less time. However, it is essential to note that speed reading should be used in places other than deep thinking and analysis. It should help you make better decisions more quickly and efficiently, but it will never replace deep thinking and analysis.

It is also essential to gradually improve your reading speed and ensure that your comprehension remains intact. Many speed reading techniques can help you improve your reading speed while maintaining a high level of understanding, such as reading aloud, diagonally, using visual markers, etc. Using these techniques strategically; you can significantly increase your reading speed while maintaining a high level of comprehension.

Analyze information critically using speed reading.

Critical thinking is a paramount quality in today's world, where we are constantly bombarded with information from different sources. Critical thinking allows you to question the information you receive and critically analyze it to determine its validity and relevance.

To develop critical thinking skills, asking questions about what you read or hear is essential. This helps you better understand the author's or speaker's point of view and determine whether or not their arguments are sound. You should also be able to evaluate the sources of information you use. This means checking the reliability and credibility of these sources and ensuring that the facts they present are accurate.

Finally, thinking independently about what you read or hear is important. Don't take what you read or hear for granted, but do your research and reflect on what you have learned to reach your conclusions. This will help you develop critical thinking skills and become more independent.

Combining critical thinking and speed reading allows you to process information efficiently and make better decisions. Here are some tips for developing your necessary thinking skills and improving your reading speed:

Ask questions: when you read something, ask yourself questions about what you read. What is the author trying to say? Why are they saying it this way? What are the author's arguments?

Evaluate information sources: It is essential to check the reliability and credibility of your information sources. Be sure to read quality sources and check the facts before deciding.

Think independently: don't take for granted what you read or hear. Think independently and make your conclusions.

Using these tips, you can develop critical thinking skills and improve reading speed. You can make better decisions and understand the information presented to you more thoroughly.

Identify critical information for quick and effective decision-making.

We are constantly bombarded with much information from different sources, and it can be challenging to find the time to read it all. However, it is crucial to understand that you can read only some things to make good decisions. In fact, by learning to identify the essential information in a text, you can focus on that information and make better decisions more quickly.

To identify the most important information in a text, you can use speed reading techniques such as skimming or selective reading. These techniques allow you to quickly locate essential information and main ideas and read them first.

It is also essential to develop your overall understanding of the information. This means understanding the context in which the information is presented and how it fits into the larger picture of what you already know about the topic. You will better understand the information and make better decisions by developing your overall understanding.

It is important to note that every book is different, and there is no rule about what to read first. However, here are some things to consider when deciding what to read first in a book:

- The title and subtitle: The title and subtitle of the book can give you an idea of what to expect in the book and what will be most important.

- Table of Contents: The book's table of contents gives you an overview of the book's structure and lets you know where the most critical information is.

- Introduction and Chapter 1: The introduction and chapter 1 of the book can give you an idea of the author's purpose and the general organization.

- Summaries and summaries: Some books include summaries or summaries that give you an overview of the most critical information.

Manage stress and make decisions quickly with speed reading

Stress management is essential to maintain a good mental and physical balance. In stressful situations, staying focused and making good decisions is often difficult. This is where speed reading can help.

It can be helpful in stressful situations because it allows you to take in information more quickly, which can help you manage stress better and make better decisions quickly.

There are several speed-reading techniques, such as reading aloud, skimming, or reading by following keywords. These techniques can help you better understand and remember the content and focus on what is essential.

By using speed reading, you can also improve your ability to make good decisions quickly. By taking in information more quickly, you have more time to think and evaluate your options. This can help you make better decisions, even in stressful or pressured situations.

It is important to note that speed reading takes practice and patience. It can be challenging to master at first, but with continued practice, you can improve your reading speed and use it to manage stress better and make better decisions quickly in stressful situations.

CONCLUSION

What is next?

This book on speed reading is worth emphasizing the importance of regular practice to maintain and improve one's speed reading skills. Indeed, as with any skill, standard practice is crucial to preserving and enhancing speed reading performance. It may seem obvious, but it is easy to overlook the importance of training when developing new skills. However, it is through regular exercise that you will see your progress accelerate, and you will be able to apply the techniques and tips in this book.

Speed reading can be a valuable tool for saving time, staying informed, and making better decisions in your daily life. However, finding the time to practice regularly and put the techniques and tips you've learned into practice can be difficult. Fortunately, there are several ways to incorporate speed reading into your life practically and efficiently.

First, you can use speed reading whenever you read articles, books, or newspapers. You don't need to dedicate specific time to speed reading every day. Instead, you can use the techniques you have learned every time you read something. This will help you improve your skills naturally and make speed reading a more accessible part of your life.

You can also use online tools to help you practice speed reading. Some many sites and apps offer speed reading exercises and tests to help you improve your skills. You can use these tools to practice conveniently and quickly without having to dedicate specific time to speed reading every day.

Finally, you can also use speed reading to help you manage your time more efficiently. If you have many documents to read or emails to go through, you can use speed-reading techniques to read them faster and save time. This will allow you to manage your time better and focus on the most critical tasks.

It is also important to remember that speed reading is not just about speed but also comprehension. By following the techniques and tips presented in this book, you should be able to read faster while maintaining a good understanding of what you are reading.

Finally, remember that speed reading is a skill like any other and, like any skill, requires time and practice to develop and improve. So don't be discouraged if you don't see immediate progress, and keep practicing regularly. You will see your speed reading skills improve dramatically with time and practice.

So I wish you well on your journey to faster reading and better understanding. Remember, speed reading can help you save time, stay informed, and make better decisions in your daily life. So, practice the techniques and tips we've covered in this book and immediately enjoy the benefits of speed reading.

Printed in Great Britain
by Amazon